SIX KEYS TO UNLOCKING YOUR DOOR OF GREATNESS

MIKE O. NWANGWA

authorHOUSE®

AuthorHouse™ UK
1663 Liberty Drive
Bloomington, IN 47403 USA
www.authorhouse.co.uk
Phone: 0800 047 8203 (Domestic TFN)
*   +44 1908 723714 (International)*

Published by AuthorHouse 09/20/2019

ISBN: 978-1-7283-9362-9 (sc)
ISBN: 978-1-7283-9363-6 (e)

Dedication

Pelumi, Peace and Niyi Adeyemo

Daniella and Michaela Oyelere

Reuel. Roniel and Ranen Adeniyi-Suberu

Alexander and Winston Ogechi

Greatness has been unlocked for you!

CONTENTS

INTRODUCTION

Have you ever been stranded because you took the wrong keys and only discovered when you got to your car or home?

You may have a bunch of keys, yet not be able to open a door if the keys are not the right one for *that* door.

In this book, I take you through six keys that would literally change your life and help you attain heights you so desire. Six keys that, if used, well will unlock every door for you.

Whether you want money, a job, happiness, a relationship or just some confidence, this book will help you achieve them.

It doesn't matter how fortified a door is. With the right key, you'll gain entrance easily.

I present to you *Six Keys To Unlocking Your Door Of Greatness.*

Mike.

I'M COMING TO THE TOP

I know you think I'm crazy
Or that I'm just dreaming.
But I mean every word of this—
'I'm coming to the top!'

I may not have much money now.
Never mind my two shirts and pair of trousers
I know I'm homeless now
At best, a squatter
Okay, so what! Everybody knows I can't
Afford to eat well.
It's very obvious from my pale face
And rather elongated neck.
But I dare say this today—
'I'm coming to the top!'

My dreams are bigger than me
And my vision, my pocket can't contain.
But that's the way it should be
Else, we'd all die of stagnation.
Going by what I see now,
It will be easier for an elephant
To pass through the eye of a needle,
Than for my dreams to come true.
But going by what I don't see
Going by God's promise,
I know my desires will come to pass.

My beginning is truly humble
I don't think any situation could be humbler
Than mine right now.
But I tell you what—
'I'm coming to the top!'

To the left and to the right,
Above, beneath and around.
I sense this darkness…
Darkness of limitations, past failures,
Fear and doubt.
The darkness is so thick, I can almost
Touch it.

But I see through the darkness.
I see light, the light of God's word.
His word is a lamp, and His promises a light.
Now I see!
I look beyond my present state
To what God says I will be.
My dreams and desires will be fulfilled,
The helplessness and hopelessness of
My present state, notwithstanding.
So with joy in my heart and full
Assurance of victory,
I yell unreservedly—
'I'm coming to the top!'

#KEY 1

DON'T LET ANYONE WRITE YOU OFF. NOTHING IS WRITTEN UNTIL YOU WRITE IT.

WRITTEN OFF

Have you ever felt that you have been written off by people? It can be really painful, especially when it comes from close family members or people you really respect. Sometimes, people don't come out plainly to tell you they think you are a write-off, but you see it in their eyes when you talk about your dreams; you see it in their reactions when you ask them for help in one area or another of your life. To them, you are probably like a drain pipe, and everything invested into your life is a waste. After all, they don't expect you to succeed, so why help you in any way?

Are you the only one facing this predicament? No sir! Many others are in the same boat as you and countless others before you passed through the same challenge. I will take you through the lives of several people who were written off, yet succeeded in spite of it all.

GIDEON

Gideon was a write-off as far as leadership was concerned. Even he knew it and so declared in vs. 15 of Judges 6: (NIV)

> **"Pray, Lord, how can I deliver Israel? Behold my clan is the weakest in Manasseh and I am the least in my family."**

God was calling Gideon to deliver Israel from the Midianites but he remembered he was a write-off. It had probably been rammed into his brain from childhood that he couldn't make a difference in this dog-eat-dog world. However, God thought differently. God encouraged him to –

> **"Go with the strength you have and rescue Israel from the Midianites. I am sending you. "**
>
> (Judges 6:14 N.L.T)

Now wait a minute! Don't we sometimes wait to have all the strength, time, resources, connections et cetera before embarking on a venture? From here, I see that if we wait to have it all, we may never accomplish anything meaningful on earth. There are no ideal situations, we create them. God said to Gideon: *go with the strength you have; you don't need all the strength in the world. All you need is me with you. I am your strength.* So, all you need too is God with you. He will help you achieve more with the little time, small strength, sparse connections; you have than those that seem to have it all. Just trust Him. God saw the strength Gideon had even though Gideon himself hadn't seen it then.

Gideon went on to put an end to the oppression of Israel by Midian. How did such a write-off rise to prominence? He began to see that no man is born a write-off. It is people that turn other people into write-offs. It is individuals that accept and believe the lie that they are write-offs. But once the written-off decide that they will change their status, they rise to be great vessels in God's hands. Gideon's real strength was dependence on God. (Judges 6:7&8)

KING DAVID

Great men seem to be talked about all the time. No one wastes time talking about nonentities. It makes ones jawbones ache. It is more worthwhile talking about great men. But we seem to forget, sometimes, that every great man was one time unknown. David was not an exception. As a young boy, he looked after his father's sheep. He was a committed shepherd boy for he risked his life fighting a bear at one time, and a lion at another, just to save his sheep.

In 1Samuel 16, we see what happened when the prophet Samuel went to Jesse's house to anoint Israel's new king. David's father made all his sons who were home pass before Samuel and would probably not have bothered about David if Samuel had not asked if those were all his sons. It was then Jesse (David's father) said his youngest son (David) was the only one left, but he was out keeping the sheep. If it had been important to Jesse, don't you think he'd have sent for David to pass before Samuel, just like the others did? Is it possible that even David's father had written him off? Maybe he saw David as good material for a shepherd. But for a king? No way; tall order! Thank God who doesn't write us off. God looks at the heart and not our size, age, beauty, fluency, wealth or gait. None of those people in Jesse's house sat down until David, the write-off, arrived from the fields. I don't know for how long they waited, standing. Father, sons and prophet all stood waiting for little David, the written-off shepherd boy. (1 Samuel 16:1-13)

As soon as David arrived, Samuel anointed him king. Ray Boltz, the inspiring singer couldn't have put it better in his song: '*When others see a shepherd boy, God may see a King.*' so what do you see in your own life? It's not just what people think of you that matters; it's what you think of yourself and what God thinks of you.

JEPHTHAH

Have you ever been insulted by anyone? I'll take it further now—has anyone ever insulted your parents? Wondering what I'm up to? But has your mother ever been called a whore? Now I bet if anyone ever did that, you didn't just smile and thank them for the compliment. None of us would like our mother being called a prostitute. Furthermore, none of us would be proud to be the child of a prostitute. But Jephthah was born by a harlot. His father's name was Gilead. Gilead had a legal wife who had sons for him. Jephthah grew up in his father's house but at a point, the sons of the legitimate wife threw him out of the house. They were afraid he would share in their father's inheritance (it's amazing how people struggle for inheritance. Sometimes it seems like they can hardly wait for their parents or relatives to die so they could inherit their wealth.). The painful reality is that Jephthah was thrown out of his own father's house. He was turned overnight into a homeless wanderer, a castaway, a refugee. He was a write-off! And the interesting thing is that there is no record that his father protested. Did he also share the write-off opinion with Jephthah's brothers? Who knows?

Jephthah fled to the land of Tob and there, some worthless fellows or band of rebels made him their leader. After a time, Israel was attacked by the Ammonites so the elders of Gilead went looking for Jephthah to come fight for them (he must have had great success with that band of rebels). Jephthah, the one time write-off was now the one calling the shots. He told them he would fight for them only on one condition—that they make him their ruler. They had no choice. They agreed. Judges chapters 11 & 12 tell the story of Jephthah. He became ruler over those who threw him out. He defeated the Ammonites and freed Israel from their oppressive rule. So much for a write-off.

Jephthah did not withdraw into his shell after being cast out of his own father's house. He did not organize a pity party and feed himself on 'roast sorrow' or 'fried regret'. He did not sit, lamenting his wretched, pitiful, pathetic fate. Instead he went to another town and got himself busy. I don't encourage you to go raiding people like he did with his group, but we can learn from him in that he exercised his gift of administration. He was such a good leader that he successfully headed a group of rebels (if you think that was easy, see if you can try it sometime).

Jephthah was also a born fighter. He made a success of his little gang. Note the introduction at the beginning of Judges 11: 'Now Jephthah the Gileadite was a mighty warrior...' That's the way God saw him—as a mighty warrior, not as a prostitute's son. Don't die a nervous wreck when you were born to be a warrior. Stop seeing yourself as a write-off. Allow the warrior in you to come alive. And do you know what the name *Jephthah* means? It is Hebrew for *'Jehovah will open'*. I pray for you, dear friend, that Jehovah will open doors that have hitherto been shut against you. Jehovah will open the doors that have shut you in or shut you out and made you feel like a write-off. Jehovah will open those doors and you will emerge from them like Jephthah, a mighty warrior.

ZACCHAEUS

Zacchaeus was a wealthy man. He was the chief tax collector. He most likely, resided in Jericho because Luke 19:1-2 tells us that Jesus was passing through Jericho when Zacchaeus met him. I'm sure Zacchaeus was a household name in his town. He was a brand; a regrettable one. The people always talked about him, but not for good. In fact he seemed to be public enemy. Tax collectors then were not exactly loved by the masses. There was no love lost between them and the masses because they cheated and extorted money from people. They fattened their purses at the people's expense. Zacchaeus was considered a sinner by the people. If you'd been living in his time, you'd have thought so too. Yet as we read his story in Luke 19:1-9, we see that he had a heart for God. He wanted to see Jesus more than those who felt they were more deserving of God. He was a tax collector, yes. He lived fat on the misery of others, true. But he wanted to meet with Jesus.

Mr. Zacchaeus was a write-off as far as the people were concerned. He was a bad man, but God saw things differently. Zacchaeus yearned for change. He was short, so he couldn't see Jesus because of the crowd. But he was unperturbed by the crowd trouble; he ran ahead and climbed a sycamore tree so that he could at least catch a glimpse of Jesus as He passed by. What humility! Remember he was a big shot in town. I wonder if our big shots today would do that. But Zacchaeus threw caution to the wind, and position to the birds for he was about to meet the king of kings. He was a sinner, a write-off. Yes; he knew that but that was why he needed, all the more, to see Jesus. Tax collector Zacchaeus was hungry for change. He desired a divine touch. Can you imagine how Zacchaeus felt when Jesus looked up at him in the tree and, calling him by name, declared that He would stay in the tax collector's house that day? What honor!

It was a jubilant, exuberant Zacchaeus that came down from that sycamore tree that day. He had climbed the tree a sinner, alien to God but now he came down to meet with the one who forgives sins. Of course the people complained that Jesus was going to be the guest of a sinner. But

Jesus didn't bother, neither did Zacchaeus. They were just expressing their opinion. Sometimes people who fail to receive from God become envious of those who get blessed. But that ought not to be. Rather than complain, thank God for what He is doing in the lives of others and God will in turn give you many reasons to celebrate. That day, Zacchaeus stood and declared to Jesus that he would give half of his possessions to the poor and that he would pay back four-fold whatever he had defrauded anybody of. What sacrifice! What genuine repentance! (See Ezekiel 33:14-16)

Some people make a living by cheating others. Some folks hold on to other people's possessions. They don't want to let go because they fear they will become poorer if they give the rightful owners their belongings. But that view is distorted. You don't get rich by taking other people's things; you get rich by giving out your own things. So like Zacchaeus, please return whatever you have unlawfully or unfairly acquired. Don't make it a habit to hold on to other people's possession. It is covetousness and it is a sin. Jesus said to Zacchaeus, 'Today salvation has come to this house…' Zacchaeus was saved that day. If he continued with his decision to live a new life, he'd have been an honest tax collector from that day on. I believe he'd have helped sanitize the 'tax-collecting industry'.

Zacchaeus' status changed that day from write-off to God's son. *Zacchaeus* in Greek means '*Pure*'. He was born to be pure, to live for God but he was living as a sinner. Thank God he met Jesus and got changed to what he was born to be. You too can meet Jesus. You too can be changed to pure; no matter how sinful you are right now. If you really need change, He is willing to help you. Reach out to Jesus. Call out to Him; tell Him to help you, to save you; he will change your name from 'sinner' to 'pure'.

THE TRUE WORTH OF A TALENT.

In Matthew 25:14-30 we read a story popularly called: the parable of the talents. Jesus told of a man going on a journey who gave his servants money to invest for him while he was away. We are told the man gave one of his servants five talents, another two talents, and one talent to the third servant. Scripture makes us understand that the money was given to them according to their abilities. Somebody is probably wondering, 'Why hasn't God called me to preach like Billy Graham; or sing like Shirley Caesar or prophesy like Elijah?' all I'll tell you is, God knows your abilities. He knows what you can do. He knows what he has packaged you for. Rather than grumble, appreciate whatever deposit or ability God has placed within you and be faithful in using it. As you prove yourself faithful in little things, God will entrust you with much more.

One of the servants invested his five talents and gained five more; the second man traded with his two talents and gained two more. But the third servant dug a hole and hid his one talent. I have always wondered why the master gave him only one talent. After all, one talent was too small for him to do anything. You probably think so too. But over the years, I've come to know better. A talent is not as worthless as you may think. The new living translation replaces '*talent*' with '*bag of gold*'. So that guy buried a bag of gold. All he saw was just one talent. In Bible times, 50 *shekels* were equal to 1 *mina* and 60 *minas* were equal to 1 *talent*. Now a mina is equivalent to 3months' wages of a laborer. So one talent was 60 minas x 3months' wages which amounts to 180 months' or 15 years' wages of a laborer. Can you beat that? That man was given 1 talent—the sweat of a laborer for 15 years…and he buried it!

Do not belittle your talent. Don't bury it like that servant. Don't write yourself off. Don't give excuses why you cannot put your talent to use. It is worth a lot more than you think. Your little talent can touch more lives than you can imagine; it can break down barriers and accomplish what others with 'mega gifts' cannot accomplish. Look within you and begin to see the power in your talent. Moses didn't think much of his rod at first, Gideon didn't think much of his strength, David's father didn't think much of him; neither did Jephthah's family. But all these people rose to prominence when they learnt to see themselves as achievers, even though situation seemed to suggest they were write-offs. You are a lot bigger than what you think.

What is the true worth of a talent? It is worth what you make it worth. It is worth what it accomplishes. It is worth the faithfulness with which you put it to use.

POPULAR BUT NOT GREAT.

We often mistake popular for great
Just like we mistake an empty boast for faith.
But just as night is different from day
So popularity and greatness differ in every way

To be popular is just to be known
Whether for good or evil by everyone
But the great are those who have shown
Others the path to greatness, one by one.

The popular may soon be forgotten after they're gone
For the thrill they once produced often dies with them
But the great are never forgotten even when they're worn
For they have lived to make out of every being, a rare gem.

Greatness is measured by your impact on lives
And not necessarily by what men say of you
For you could be popular and end up in the archives
What I tell you now is really true.

#KEY 2

GET YOUR DEFINITION OF SUCCESS AND FAILURE RIGHT. LET GOD, NOT PEOPLE DEFINE IT FOR YOU.

REDEFINING SUCCESS AND FAILURE

The general idea most people have about being successful is being rich and occupying an important position. A failure would be considered as one who is poor or has not achieved much especially when compared with other 'successful' people. God views success and failure differently. A success in God's eyes is not just the person with loads of money, cars, houses, land, investments and other material things. True success, from God's viewpoint is simply fulfilling the purpose of God for your life. Success is reaching out to someone and making that person's life better. Success is not in the magnitude of what you have accomplished or acquired, it is in doing what God would have you do. Sometimes it's hard for us as humans to see things from God's point of view. No wonder many try so hard to acquire as much as possible for themselves. They make it look like they are in some form of competition with others as they try to grab for themselves as much material things as they can. In Leo Tolstoy's story: *how much land does a man need?* He makes us understand that if we take a moment to think about it, we'll discover that when we die, all we'll require is a grave six-foot deep.

Even if we get real dressed-up, bedecked with expensive jewelry and are put in a golden casket, it won't change the fact that we are dead and we won't be able to take our wealth, houses, fleet of cars and laurels with us. We won't be able to appreciate the befitting burial our children and loved ones have arranged for us, neither would we be able to thank all the guests for coming to pay their last respect. Pretty pathetic, isn't it? If that is the case, then we should really begin to look for lasting success—something we can take with us when we die. We need to look for something we can go to God's presence with and which God Himself will regard as success. Like what? Well, like the assurance of having fulfilled God's purpose for your life; of having made an impact on the lives of people; of having been a representative of God on earth, wiping tears from people's eyes and showing them what it means to be loved and cared for.

How do we relate success and failure to fulfilling our call? If you are a pastor, for instance, with a church membership of twenty thousand people and there is another pastor somewhere down town with a 300-member church, you may be tempted to regard yourself as a very great man of God and the other pastor a 'not-so-great man of God' but that would be a very wrong line of thought. A pastor with a large church membership isn't necessarily more spiritual than a pastor with a small church membership and vice versa. However, if God were to assess them, it is the quality of their work that'll count and not the magnitude or quantity alone. Never get carried away by large membership. Don't let that be the judge or measure of your spiritual level. It could fail you utterly. On the other hand, don't think you are the only one with the true and undiluted word of God just because few people attend your church. It doesn't always follow like that. After all, John the Baptist too preached the true and undiluted word of God, yet people trooped to hear him way out in the wilderness.

So, how do we know when we are succeeding in ministry? A constant check on the original vision God gave you, as well as communion with the Holy Spirit will do. Every pastor, preacher, minister should re-assess his work. Is it all about numbers and no substance? God is more concerned with substance than numbers. Take a look at 1 Corinthians 3:11-15: (NLT)

> *'For no one can lay any other foundation than the one we already have—Jesus Christ. Now anyone who builds on that foundation may use gold, silver, jewels, wood, hay or straw. But there is going to come a time*

> *of testing at the judgment day to see what kind of work each builder has done. Everyone's work will be put through the fire to see whether or not it keeps its value. If the work survives the fire that builder will receive a reward. But if the work is burned up, the builder will survive great loss. The builders themselves will be saved, but like someone escaping through a wall of flames.'*

A thousand dollars worth of Gold will be negligible quantity-wise when compared with the same value of wood or hay. A thousand dollars worth of gold may fit into a lady's hand bag but a thousand dollars worth of wood? You'll need a truck for that. Now, let's not even try to imagine what we'll use to carry a thousand dollars worth of hay. But let all the above mentioned be subjected to intense fire and then, you'll know the must valuable. The wood and hay will be consumed but the gold will come out refined. If you want to be successful, don't just go for fame or money or big structures. Go for quality, impact, truth, and integrity. In no time, fame, money and big structures will all be yours. It is usually disheartening to hear of a preacher who operates under great anointing getting involved in a financial or moral scandal. Even if the whole city attended his church, will you still see him as a success? True success goes beyond what you have, it is what you are. This shouldn't frighten you from aspiring to do great things for God, instead watch out for quality as there are many pressures on your way to the top to start chasing shadows rather than things of value.

MOSES, THE MAN WHO OWNED A LARGE FLOCK

> *'Now Moses was keeping the flock of his father-in-law Jethro, the priest of Midian, and he led his flock to the west side of the wilderness and came to Horeb, the mountain of God… Come, I will send you to Pharaoh that you may bring forth my people, the sons of Israel, out of Egypt.'*
>
> *(Exodus 3:1&10 R.S.V)*

Moses was a successful shepherd. He was obviously doing well tending sheep for Jethro, his father-in-law. If you had met Moses on a typical day with his large flock, you may have tagged him a great success. God would have seen it differently, though. Moses had the capacity, the grace and the call to lead a nation. Yet he was marking time with a flock of sheep. Could that be the same with you? God has something much greater in store for you but you are operating far below capacity. In the eyes of people, you're complete and successful. You're making a lot of money; you have a lot of connections. But sincerely ask yourself this question: am I fulfilled? There is no peace or fulfillment outside God's plan for you.

God eventually reached out to Moses and gave him the call that truly belonged to him—bringing the Israelites out of bondage. Moses had tried to do that on his own forty years before by killing an Egyptian slave-driver but his failure in that campaign shows us what happens to people who try to do things on their own—they fall flat on their faces.

> '...*it **is not by strength that one prevails.***
> **(1 Sam 2:9b N.I.V)**

It doesn't matter the size of your flock. If you are not doing what God wants you to do, you're a failure. To know more about Moses, read chapters 2 and 3 of Exodus.

GOOD AND BAD SUCCESS

> '***This book of the law shall not depart out of your mouth, but you shall meditate on it day and night, that you may be careful to do according to all that is written in it; then you shall make your way prosperous, and then you shall have good success.***'
> **(Joshua 1:8 R.S.V)**

This was God's challenge to Joshua. Now it is God's challenge to you and me. True success begins by studying God's word, meditating on it and putting it to practice. Some folks can tell you everything God says but won't obey any of it themselves. The area I want to underscore here is what God says to Joshua about being prosperous and having 'good success.' I am convinced from this that there's something called 'bad success'. Else God would have simply said: '*…you shall have success*'

One time God told Moses to speak to the rock so that water could come from it; Moses got angry with the people and struck the rock instead. Did water come forth from the rock? Oh yes! And the people drank their fill. They probably composed a song of praise that day as they were wont to do when things were going well. It was success as far as they were all concerned but to God it was not 'good Success' it was 'bad Success'. (See Numbers 20:1-13)

Have you ever heard of one king Solomon? He is about the wisest man that ever lived. God gave him unequaled wisdom and wealth because he chose the service of God and wisdom to lead God's people above material things. Solomon was so blessed that Jesus used him as an example in one of his homilies. (Matt. 6:28-30). Solomon did very well as a king. There was no war in his time. As far as I know, Solomon fought no war. But as time went on, the king began to marry women of idolatrous cultures. Women, then, were a token of political alliances. If king A married the daughter of king B, it was a guarantee there'd be no war between both kingdoms. Solomon made a lot of alliances to boost foreign relations. And the number of wives he had was a proof of how good his foreign relations was—700 wives.

The foreign women Solomon married introduced idol worship into Israel. Solomon was rich and wise but he and his wives had become a snare to Israel. He ended up with 700 wives and 300 concubines. Quite a number for one man! That, to some people, is probably an indication of success. But sorry, it was 'bad success.'

Some men think the number of wives they marry reflects their status as successful people. All I'll say to such is that they take a cue from Solomon. He was an expert in women's affairs. He wouldn't think the way you're thinking now if he had a second chance. Solomon ended up straying from God. His good success of wealth and wisdom metamorphosed into bad success of chronic polygamy and idolatry. Bad success is another name for failure. So if you want to succeed, watch out for bad success; only a thin line separates it from good success.

A LITTLE MORE ON SUCCESS

Being a celebrity does not make you a success. Walt Disney was once asked by a reporter how it felt to be a celebrity. "It feels fine," he said, 'when being a celebrity helps me to get a choice reservation for a football game. As far as I remember, being a celebrity has never helped me to make a good picture, or a good shot at a polo game, or command the obedience of my daughter, or impress my wife. It doesn't help me to keep fleas off our dogs and if being a celebrity won't give me advantage over a couple of fleas, then I guess there can't be that much in being a celebrity after all.' You may be a celebrity and fail in your home, in your character or in blessing the lives God intends you to bless. It is not an evil thing to be celebrated. It is whether you are doing what God has called you to do, the way He has called you to do it that counts; it is what goes on in your heart, your motives for doing whatever you do. Those, and not what people say, are the criteria God will assess you with. Check out the following scriptures: Proverbs 10:2, 22; Proverbs 21:6; Proverbs 28:16.

The bottom line is that true success begins with the fear of God. Not fear in terms of dread. But fear in terms of awe and respect mixed with love. If we truly love God and are more concerned about what He thinks and how He wants us to carry out our call, or run our business; if we concentrate on making impact in our generation, speaking the truth, walking in integrity, helping those God gives us the grace to assist, then even if the world does not see us as successful, God does. Whose opinion matters more to you? God's or the world's?

STRUGGLING

If you find yourself having difficulties or facing challenges as regards your call, business or project, please do not give up. You may have tried several times and failed, but please do not give up. The future may look bleak now but it isn't bleak. God will make a way. If He is the one who has inspired you to do what you are doing, then He will help you succeed. You may think too that your efforts are unappreciated, unproductive or negligible but somebody somewhere is getting blessed. Keep working at it! If at the end of the day, your effort blesses a single life, you'd have done a great thing or why else would the host of heaven rejoice over one sinner who repents? (Luke 15:3-7).

To round off this chapter, I'll tell you the story of a Baptist preacher called Mordecai Hamm. He'd just concluded a 3-week revival in North Carolina and he left town discouraged because nobody was won to Christ, save for one 12-year old boy. Will you consider that outing a failure or a success? Before you answer, let me tell you what the young boy's name is—Billy Graham! Yeah! It was he. Billy Graham turned out to be one of the greatest evangelists of the twentieth century. Billy Graham has shared the Gospel with several United States presidents and mammoth crowds have accepted Jesus Christ in his crusades. Thanks to Mordecai Hamm. And thanks to God for using Mordecai Hamm.

So when next you think Billy Graham, think Mordecai Hamm. By the way, do you still think Mordecai's revival meeting was a flop?

GREAT FAITH

I'll tell you the story of 'Faith-full' Felix
Who had great faith but lacked the works
He'd sit down all day and boast to us:
One day I will go to Sydney, Rome, and Venice
None dared challenge him
Lest we be said to have no faith
But while we worked hard with zest and vim
Felix did no work but wait on faith.

How would one eat if he does no work?
How would one be rich without working for it?
But Felix, 'Mr. Faith-full' would not hear of it
He'd rather let his faith do the work.
He'd fast and pray and groan and wail
Felix was getting it all wrong
For faith without works is sure to fail
Such faith isn't much better than cow dung

Today, I make this known to you
I've been to Sydney, Rome, and Venice
But my dear 'Faith-full' Felix
Has had to start life anew
After years of faith without works
He's just now learning to do it right
Life has given him a few knocks
All because of his folly. Sorry plight.

Felix never got to cross
The nearest river to our village
But now he knows faith is just a visual image
Of your desires, goals and course
Faith will help you focus on your desires
But without works, faith is sterile and dead
Works are what your faith requires
To make it from point A to Z.

#KEY 3

NO MAN HAS A MONOPOLY ON GREATNESS. YOU TOO CAN BE GREAT IF YOU SO DESIRE.

THE QUEST FOR GREATNESS

We all want to become great. Yet greatness is not thrust on people. A dear brother in my church said: 'Greatness is not in the blood.' When I thought of it, I knew it was a great truth. We work towards greatness. It is God that makes men great, so He's the first person you must contact. Ask Him to help you, ask Him to give you the secrets of greatness. Ask Him to bring your way people that will aid you to greatness. Then read, study, research and soon you'll find the way. In addition you can learn from the following points. There are things you must do and avoid if you really want to be great. Let's take a look at a couple of them.

1. *BE HUMBLE ENOUGH TO START SMALL:*

   The reason we don't have more great men today is that many people don't want to start small. No man is born great. But men work their way to greatness. There is no great man today who was not once small. We are not the achievers we desire to be simply because we don't want to start from the scratch. We all love a finished job. Everyone wants to be part of the success story but not many want to be part of the building process, the failure phase or the foundational phase. If you must accomplish this great vision of yours, then put your gifts to work little by little. You have to go through the stage of smallness. Anyone who skips past that stage in a bid to hurriedly get to the top will come back to it at one point or another in their lives. A wise man said, 'whatever I know at the top, I learnt at the bottom.'

Those who stumble into greatness oftentimes stumble out of it. Some men achieve greatness but lose it with time. This is so because they have not been trained to handle smallness. By all means, do not neglect your days of small beginnings. No amount of money or formal training will teach you the experience people gain from small beginnings. The only way to get that experience is to earn it. And how is that possible? By starting small! It was F.B Meyer that said: 'I used to think that God's gifts were placed on shelves, one above the other and that to get the best gifts, one has to climb higher. But I've found that God's gifts are placed on shelves one below the other and to get the best gifts, we need to stoop lower.'

Stoop lower! That's the key. Stoop lower in humility and serve others. Stoop lower in hard work and be fruitful in your state of smallness. It takes a great man to start small. Ask any celebrity today and if they're honest with you, they'll tell you that at one time they were virtually unknown. They were once small. But rather than die off lamenting their smallness, they appreciated it as a passageway to the top. They worked hard, and were consistent in what they were doing and it was just a matter of time before they were being celebrated. Perhaps no one is celebrating you today. But could you just take your mind off being celebrated and focus on what God has called you to do? There's nothing special in being celebrated. What is really special is being fulfilled and successful. If people celebrate you and you feel empty and unfulfilled, note that the latter will negate the former. There is nothing more special than receiving God's approval in your work and knowing that you have blessed someone's life. Be faithful in your days of small beginnings. Don't be discouraged. Ignore the mocking; you will get to the top. But please never forget that to get to the top of the ladder, you can't by-pass the rungs.

> ***'And though you start with little, you will end with much.'***
>
> **(Job 8:7 N.L.T)**

'And though your beginning was small, your latter days will be very great.'

(R.S.V)

2. DON'T BE SCARED OF FAILURE:

It is said that some people never fail because they never try. A man who has failed in the process of trying is a lot wiser than one who has never failed, but has never tried either. Many today are scared of failing and that's why they have not moved forward. If you must fulfill God's call for your life, you must first overcome the fear of failure. You are not ready for success until you accept that great successes are achieved in spite of failures and not in the absence of them. Maybe you have failed several times and you are about to call it quits, you think you are a failure. You think you were born to lose, born to fail but I have a different idea. I think you are not a failure. You may have failed but that doesn't make you a failure.

A man who had things going quite well for him was suddenly laid-off from work. It came as a big shock to him. He was demoralized. He got home that day and began to weep before his wife. He showed her the sack letter and said to her: 'I'm a failure.' Thank God for good, supportive wives. She looked him in the eye and said, 'Honey, you're not a failure. Failure is an *event* and not a person.' That is real truth, folks. You and I are not failures; we may only have experienced failure. A boss told his subordinate, 'Don't tell them we failed. Tell them we decided to temporarily postpone our success.' Never give in.

History is replete with men who encountered failures en route to greatness. Thomas Edison, Walt Disney, the Wright brothers, J.F Kennedy etc. it is not whether you fail that matters; it is what happens after that. Henry Ford said: 'Failure is only an opportunity to begin again, more intelligently.' Stop brooding over your failures, look for a better way to put your dream to work.

'Do not gloat over me, my enemy. Though I have fallen, I will rise...'

(Micah 7:8 N.L.T)

> **'For though a righteous man falls seven times, he rises again.'**
>
> **(Prov. 24:16 N.I.V)**

3. DARE TO TRY:

A young man told me some years back that he would have loved to go to a particular tertiary institution but did not apply for it because he was told that people rarely pass the examination taken to gain entry into the school. I told him he should never have believed such talk. Wasn't it possible that if only five people passed that exam, he could be one of them? He saw my point that day. But, of course, he had lost that opportunity. Don't let anyone convince you not to try because a particular project is very difficult. Refuse to listen to anyone who tells you that you cannot achieve your dream because you are young or because only few people have done it before you. Except you try, you will never know your ability. And even if you fail, you'd be the better for it. You'd have conquered the fear of failure.

In 1 Samuel 17, we read about the young man, David. He had gone to take some food to his brothers, and, seeing the ridicule the Israelites were subjected to by Goliath and the Philistines, he decided to fight Goliath. Note that everyone, including the King, was afraid to challenge the philistine warrior, Goliath. But a young lad, that day dared to tread the path even his fathers had been too frightened to tread. A young lad dared to be a trail blazer. He did something no one had ever done before—defeat Goliath. But I must let you know, again, that he did not try by his might. He declared in verse 45: 'You come to me with sword, spear and javelin, but I come to you in the name of the Lord Almighty—the God of the armies of Israel whom you have defiled.'

What happened that day is now history. Goliath fell, all because David dared to venture out in the name of the LORD. Could God be saying something to you now? Step out in faith. Take a step! Try out the armor God has given you. Like David, try out your sling and stones. They may not look so good especially when compared with other types of weapons. But guess what? They're good enough to bring down Goliath! I know you can do it. Just dare to try. It was Rev. Jersey Jackson who said: *'If I try, I may fail. But if I don't try, I will always fail.'*

4.   *BE WILLING TO EMBRACE CHANGE*:

It is often said that the only thing that will not change is change itself. As long as this world remains, change will continue to take place. The questions to answer are: what will be your response to change? Will change leave you better off or worse off? Will you yield to good change or bad change? There is a Chinese adage which says: 'when the wind of change begins to blow, some people build windmills, others build walls.' Some people take advantage of change and they reach great heights while others resist change to their own peril.

Is it possible to have a world that does not change? Not in this life time, it is only God who doesn't change (Malachi 3:6). That's why He is called the unchanging changer. But even at that, God *does* change His mind on issues. His personality, His principles, His word, His justice, righteousness and attributes in general will never change. But you know what? God does change His mind. He lets mercy overrule judgment many times, for instance, if not, you and I would have been dead long ago–consumed by fire and brimstone. God turns His hand of judgment over a people and lets mercy prevail (see Jonah 1-3).

In Isaiah 38:1-7 and 2 Kings 20: 1-11, prophet Isaiah was sent by God to tell King Hezekiah to prepare for death as he wouldn't recover from his sickness. The scriptures tell us that on hearing that, Hezekiah turned his face to the wall, and cried out to God to reverse His declaration upon him. God heard Hezekiah's prayer and while Isaiah was still on his way out of the palace, God sent him back to tell Hezekiah that fifteen more years had been added to his life. If God changes his mind on issues like this, it's amazing that some human beings choose to be merciless and unforgiving. When their heart is made up, it is all set like concrete. No wonder some hearts have to be broken sometimes for God to effect His will. It is not a crime to change or to embrace change, as long as it pleases God and it is for good. God changed His mind for good—in order to let men who were destined for death have abundant life.

How does this affect us? Well, we will keep having the results we've always had if we keep on doing the things we've always done. We need to ask God for insight. We ought to allow Him show us those areas of our lives, work, ministry, business or family relationships where we need to apply the principle of change. Please, this calls for balance. There is a place for consistency (doing a particular thing continually with importunity until you see results.) but there is a place for change, reorganizing your methods or overhauling your ideology completely. Only God will help you find this balance. Pray to Him and He will teach you Himself or lead you to people who will. For your vision to be fulfilled and in order for you to be successful at what you do, be sensitive to God's Spirit so that you will know when change becomes necessary.

5. *STRIVE FOR UNITY AND BROTHERHOOD*:

There is somebody out there that has what you need and there is somebody too that needs what you have. The principle above is demonstrated each time we walk into a store to buy something. We need their goods and they need our money. The key point is, both the buyers and sellers need each other. God uses people, most times to bring us to the place He has prepared for us. What we must always remember is that God is the real helper. The people He uses are just tools in His hands to help us. As a result, the real credit should go to God.

God has put so many people around us. They are great assets! We've probably not noticed, but they are all over the place—in class, in the market, in our neighborhood, on our street, in church, in that bus, in the keep-fit club etc. God can use them to promote us in different ways. It could be with as little as a suggestion or an idea they give us. Some ideas are worth a fortune. Promotion does not always come by people giving us money or contracts or material things. It could come by us giving out money and other good things to people. Give your time, energy, skill and resources to make someone's life better and God will in turn promote you.

Grace plus Grace

I heard somebody say once: 'there's enough space in the sky for all the stars to shine.' In other words, the brightness of one star does not in any way diminish another star's capacity to shine. If we understood this, then we'd quit being envious of people or fighting each other for positions. We will, instead, appreciate the blessings God has bestowed on others and celebrate with them. As we do that, we will be watering the path for our own promotion. Don't be intimidated by another person's success. If you know who you are, you won't be jealous of other people.

There is so much rivalry and antagonism in the world today. We see it in our work places, schools, in government and unfortunately, in church. If God has truly called you, don't be caught in the trap of being at war with another person. Do not be dragged into trying to prove that another person is not called by God. Do not be in a hurry to condemn your brother before others. Instead, seek to help him overcome his inadequacies if you can. Most importantly, pray for people. It is hard to criticize or condemn someone you are genuinely praying for.

> **'What are you o great mountain? Before Zerubbabel you shall become plain; and he shall bring forward the top stone amid shouts of 'Grace, grace to it.''**
> **(Zechariah 4:7) (ESV)**

That top stone (or capstone) will be put in place with *grace plus grace*, not *grace against grace*. I mean God's grace upon my life should work in consonance with God's grace upon your life. It is grace plus grace that levels Mountains, not grace against grace. I feel anyone called of God has a measure of grace upon his/her life. If I put my grace to use, and you put your grace to use, think what will happen if we worked together! There will be no force strong enough on earth to stop us. Let's quit fighting one another, especially in Christendom. If God's grace is truly upon your life, the only way to prove it is to love others and respect God's grace upon their lives too. Learn to appreciate people. The man you ignore beside you might just be the key you need to open that door that has, hitherto, been shut against you.

6. *GET YOUR PRIORITIES RIGHT:*

Misplacement of priorities has been the bane of many people's dreams and visions. Even if God's call upon your life is so strong that people can sense it a kilometer away, you will still need to pay heed to simple wisdom of getting your priorities right. Some questions that may help you are:

a. Why am I really doing this? What are the underlying motives?
b. Is this the time to do this? Or am I doing it because someone else is doing it?
c. Can I really afford it now?
d. Is God really in support of this now?

If we ask ourselves these questions, and we give honest answers to them, we'd be on our way to getting our priorities right. Before embarking on any project, check with God first. Pray to Him and let him speak to you—in your heart, through His word, through people or through whichever way He's been speaking to you before. If God approves of your project, it automatically becomes His project. So He takes the load off you. He is then committed to seeing you through.

> **'Commit everything you do to the LORD. Trust Him, and He will help you.'**
>
> **(Psalm 37:5 N.L.T)**

There is also a place for counting the cost. Not just in financial terms, but in terms of the level of commitment your vision will require and whether at that point, you can be that committed. Sometimes, money is an issue too, for your spending will also reflect how much you believe in your vision. Jesus said: 'Where you treasure is, there your heart will be.' A look at your budget and spending so far, this year, will no doubt reveal where your heart is.

Finally there is a place for faith. If God has endorsed your plan, then He will provide all you need to accomplish it. I needed about ₦200, 000 ($1,300) to publish my first book some years ago. I did not have the money, but God had ordained it was time for it. The areas I expected help to come from turned out a disappointment. I had no option but to trust Him and He graciously brought all the help I needed my way. About the same time, I was working on my final year project in the university. It required quite an amount of money to carry out. I got some money for the project from a relative, but not for the book. Someone specifically advised me to finish with my project first before talking about book writing. It was a tough decision, but I finally put my treasure where God was leading me to—in the book. The book was published with God's intervention. He raised many people I least expected to support the work. And guess what happened? From the proceeds of the book, I had much, more than enough for my project in school. I was comfortable in final year. I just want to encourage you, God will provide. Just trust Him and do what He says. That is faith.

So friend, don't misplace your priorities. Don't buy expensive plates when you have no food. Don't buy a car when you have no place to live in. don't buy shoes when you have no clothes. My examples may be quite exaggerated, but I pray God gives you understanding on this issue.

7. *THROW OUT FEAR AND INDECISION*:

A lot of great tasks that would have changed many lives remain unattempted due to fear and indecision. Indecision is actually hinged on fear. We're afraid to decide because we are afraid we will fail. Better be a failure at something than be a success at nothing! At least when you fail, you learn one more way not to do that task. If God is really in charge of our lives, then fear shouldn't rule over us anymore.

> **'The Lord is my light and my salvation. Whom shall I fear? The LORD is the stronghold of my life; of whom shall I be afraid? ...Though a host encamp against me,**

> *my heart shall not fear; though war arise against me,*
> *yet I will be confident.'*
>
> **(Psalm 27:1, 3) R.S.V)**

Fear is not of God (2 Timothy 1:7). So ask God to help you overcome it. One way to overcome fear is to confront it. Take on those challenges that scare you and you'll discover they weren't worth being afraid of in the first place. Face them head-on and watch your confidence grow. Take a bold step! Go forward! Those who don't decide will always remain beside. Someone has said that the world stands aside to let that man pass, who knows where he is going. The time it takes you to wallow in indecision is the same time it takes another person to make it to the top, to carry out his call or to fulfill his ministry. Some people you were on the same level with you are now so far up the ladder that you can't reach them easily, simply because while they took decisive steps in their lives, you kept putting off making important decisions.

An undecided man came to Jesus in Luke 9:61: (NIV)

> *'Another said, 'Yes, Lord. I will follow you, but first*
> *let me say good-bye to my family.' But Jesus told him,*
> *'anyone who puts a hand to the plow and then looks*
> *back is not fit for the kingdom of God. "*

Don't be afraid of anything. And by all means, make up your mind on issues. Many people have died without making important decisions when it was in their power all along to do so. They have left after their demise pain, regret, sorrow and shame for their loved ones just because they put off taking a stand on issues.

8. *SOW INTO THE LIVES OF OTHERS:*

What you make happen for others, God will make happen for you. The most logical way to increase is to grab as much as possible for yourself, then think of others afterwards. But God's way is different. If you want to succeed with God's help, then you will have to start thinking of others first. Someone has said that 'Joy' stands for 'Jesus',

'Others' then 'You'. You will not get to the top (and be fulfilled) thinking of yourself alone.

> ***'Do not judge and you will not be judged. Do not condemn, and you will not be condemned. Forgive, and you will be forgiven. Give and it will be given to you. A good measure, pressed down, shaken together and running over will be poured into your lap. For with the measure you use, it will be measured to you.'***
> **(Luke 6:37-38. N.I.V)**

Jesus here was teaching on how we relate to other people. We can't help it; but whatever we do to others will ultimately be our own lot too. He was talking of judging, condemning or criticizing. If we are fond of doing it to others, it will be done to us by others. Jesus wasn't just talking about money or gifts when He spoke on giving in verse 38. He was referring to our input into the lives of others, positive or negative, in whatever form.

Whatever we do to people is a seed, which will certainly yield a harvest. When we stay conscious of that it would affect how we treat people. You will never have a successful company with loyal and faithful employees in future if you're neck-deep in embezzling funds from the place you work now. You shouldn't expect to have co-operative ministers or pastors in your church in future if you are a rebel leader or faction head in your local assembly at present. If you are an opposition leader in the church now, defying the leadership of your head pastor, then watch out, it won't be long. When you become head pastor, the same thing will happen to you.

Be happy when others succeed. Celebrate their success. If you want God to raise supporters for you when you need help, begin now by supporting others. They may not know you or appreciate your sacrifice, but God sees you. He sees in secret and He rewards openly. There is no exception to this. Be faithful and supportive in the things that have to do with others and God will raise people to do likewise for you when you need help. Sow a seed today. It may be financial or it may not. But if you need financial and material increase, begin to bless other people financially and materially.

> **'Cast your bread upon the waters. For after many days you will find it again. Give portions to seven, yes to eight for you do not know what disaster may come upon the land...sow your seed in the morning, and at evening let not your hands be idle, for you do not know which will succeed, whether this or that, or whether both will do equally well.'**
>
> **(Ecclesiastes 11:1, 2, 6. (N.I.V)**

Do for others what you would like them to do for you. This is a summary of all that is taught in the law and prophets.

THE VALLEY OF DECISION

I was sleeping in that valley
That dark, damp, demoralizing vale
Everywhere, people around me seemed to
Be climbing higher…out of the valley
Making headway in life
But there was poor little me
In the valley of decision.

I was sitting in that valley
That dangerous, debilitating, distracting vale
Every other person seemed to know where they
Were going
On my part, I was waiting for the right time
To make up my mind. To make my move
But I had started waiting for that opportunity
Twelve years earlier
Alas! There was miserable little me
Still in the valley of decision.

I was standing in the valley
That dirty, dreary, demonized vale
I had begun to see what a fool I was
One bold decision, one bold move
Could have taken me higher than I was.
My friends had soared on to the mountains
Though we all were once in the valley.
So it was, at last, hopeful, little me
Wanting out of the valley of decision.

So I climbed out of that valley
That desolate, deserted, deleterious vale
Higher and higher I climbed
As I boldly made a decision here
And took a bold step there
It wasn't as hard as I thought
I had made mountains out of my valleys
So I thought I could never climb out.
But I not only climbed out of that valley
I climbed to the peak of a mountain.
That's where I still am today.
As long as you don't decide
You'll always be beside
And when others would have reached the peak
There'll still be poor little you
Crouching in the valley of decision.

#KEY 4

WHEN YOU MISS YOUR WAY, RETRACE YOUR STEPS

In my university days, I used to see a particular car with a bumper sticker which read: 'Real men don't ask directions.' Each time I read it, I always added: '…so they often get lost.' It isn't a virtue not to ask directions. It is not a sign of masculinity or intelligence. Asking directions (especially from people who know) is the easiest means to finding your way. Questions elicit answers. One major challenge people have is retracing their steps when they've missed their way. No matter how far you walk away from where you ought to be, remember you can walk back to the point from where you missed it. I confess it is not an easy thing to do. It can be humbling and sometimes humiliating. But if it takes humiliation to put you back on the right track, then thank God for it. It is better to lose your pride and find your way than keep your pride and lose your life, all because you insist on going the wrong way.

> *'There is a way that seems right to a man, but in the end, it leads to death.'*
>
> **(Prov. 14:12. N.I.V)**

As you run with your vision, as you do what God has called you to do, and as you fulfill your call, please make allowance for mistakes. As long as you are human, you are very likely to make mistakes, what amuses me about quite a lot of people, especially, in church, is that rather than admit their mistakes, they spiritualize them instead. They'd tell you everything from how God has ordained them to how His mighty revelations and grace abound in their lives. They'd rather do all that than simply admit their mistake.

Even if God spoke to you a minute ago and you make a mistake now, please admit it. Don't blame it on God. You are not infallible; you are a treasure in an earthen vessel.

> ***'He who conceals his sins does not prosper, but whoever confesses and renounces them finds mercy.'***
> **(Prov. 28:13. N.I.V)**

So when you err, admit it and learn from your mistakes. Then retrace your steps to the point from where you missed it. I have not said this to promote mediocrity. But when you make mistake, don't crucify yourself, yet you should never justify your error. Admit it, retrace your steps and move one.

THE LOST SON

Jesus told a parable about the lost (Prodigal) son. The story can be found in Luke 15:11-27. A man had two sons and one day, the younger of them asked his father to give him his own share of the inheritance. This is very striking. When you go to your father and ask for what should be given to you in the event of his death; then you are implying that you wish him dead. Nobody collects inheritance from a father who is alive. That boy, by his request, knowingly or unknowingly was declaring his father dead. But he had a loving father. And you have a loving father too—one who does not mock you when you fall or turn you back when you call on Him. The prodigal's father divided the inheritance between the two sons.

We are told that shortly after that, the younger son got his things together and set off for a distant country and there squandered his wealth in wild living. He probably thought the money would never get finished. That is the foolishness of youth. Many of us have not outgrown this stage. If you have a lot of money, be wise enough to invest it. That is because:

> *'...riches can disappear as though they had the wings of a bird.'*
>
> **(Proverbs 23:5) (TLB)**

The young man had spent the money recklessly. But it wasn't just his money that was spent; he had spent and wasted his life on wild or loose living. Friend, don't waste your life by living recklessly. God has given you so much, just like that boy's father gave him, but you shouldn't, like him, set out to foolishly squander your inheritance (your gifts, purity, womanhood, intelligence, money, youth and your life). Be wise! Verse 14 tells us that after he had spent everything, there was a severe famine in that country and he began to be in need. There's something you must know here: the famine doesn't usually come until after you have spent everything. You may not see your emptiness and poverty until you have wasted everything.

Verse 15 and 16 tell us that the young lad went and hired himself to a local farmer who sent him to feed his pigs. He longed to eat the pods that the pigs were eating but no one gave him anything. Even pigs' pods had become a welcome meal to the prodigal. What a change in fortune! He who once had everything he needed was now feeding pigs for a living.

Verse 17 is a powerful verse. It is the first step a man or woman needs to take in retracing their steps. I'll call it the step of **Realization**. I quote from the NLT.

> *'**When he finally came to his senses, he said to himself,***
> *'At home even the hired men have food enough to spare,*
> *and here I am dying of hunger.''*

You need to start asking yourself some questions e.g. with my present stance, am I better off or worse off? Did the decision I took leave me rejoicing or regretting? You have to be honest with yourself. You have to come back to your senses. That is the first step to finding yourself back—**realization**. Jesus said to the Ephesian church in Rev. 2:4 & 5— *(NIV)* *'...you have forsaken your first love. Remember the height from which you have fallen...'*

This, we must all do if we want to move forward—remember the height from which we have fallen.

The second step is what I'll call the step of ***Decision.*** Let's hear from the prodigal son in vs. 18, 19 (NLT) –*'I will go home to my father and say 'Father, I have sinned against both heaven and you, and I am no longer worthy of being called your son. Please take me on as a hired man.'*

Some decisions are very hard but when you look at your present situation, you can't afford not to take them. The boy decided to go back to his father. He would apologize and beg to be accepted back as a servant, since he no longer deserved to be treated as a son. The devil works hard to keep you from making a decision. But when you do, he cannot stop you. He can, for instance, try to prevent you from making a decision to serve God. He may try to show you how foolish your choice for God will make you look in the eyes of your friends. But as soon as you ***Decide*** to resist him, he leaves you alone. There is power in ***Decision***.

You need to decide today.

- *Decide to go back to your family.*
- *Decide to make up with your spouse*
- *Decide to end that lawsuit*
- *Decide to apologize to your pastor*
- *Decide to forgive that person who hurt you.*
- *Decide to return that money or item you stole.*
- *Decide to end that adulterous relationship*
- *Decide to put an end to your promiscuity*
- *Decide to confess that you gave a wrong testimony against the innocent*
- *Decide to surrender your life to Christ.*

There is power in DECISION!

In verse 20, we find the third step—the step of ***Faith***. After you have realized your mistake and made a decision to right it, then you need to put what you've decided to action. You need to take a step of FAITH. I call it a step of faith because sometimes you aren't sure of what will come next. You only rest in the consolation that you're doing the right thing.

Some years ago, I read about a man who was teaching his kids about honesty. They confessed they had stolen sweets from a store when the shop owner wasn't looking. The father then told them that he too had 'stolen' tools from his former place of work. He ought to have returned them when he left that company but he didn't. That day, father and children struck a deal. They went first to the company and he explained to the relevant authorities what he'd come for, and then he gave them the tools. Afterwards, he took the kids to the shop from where they'd stolen sweets and let them explain to the shop owner what they had done and apologize to him. That's fatherhood by example, if you ask me. Some parents are still telling their children not to do everything they (the parents) are doing. Don't you know it is easier to lead by example than by mere speech? I assure you that your kids watch you more than they listen to you. The message of that story touched me deeply and I shared it with a friend. I didn't know God was telling him something through that story.

When my friend was in a particular tertiary institution, he had smuggled a book out of the library and he did not return it even after he left school. One day, he said we should go back to the library of that school to return the book. This was somewhere in the region of 7-10 years after the book was smuggled out of the library. I tell you, it took a step of faith to return that book. *Realization* and *decision* alone wouldn't have done much good. A step of faith had to follow. And take that step of faith we did!

We didn't know what to expect: embarrassment? Insult? Arrest? You never know. But we went. And contrary to our expectation, the library staff that attended to us was nice and appreciative. He thanked us for returning the book but he didn't know my friend was relieved and free by that act of returning the book. You too need to return all the things you have wrongfully acquired to the rightful owners. You need to tell the truth and stop guilt from eating you up on the inside. Do what is right and free yourself from bondage.

Now back to our prodigal son story. The second part of verse 20 tells us that while he was still a long distance away, his father saw him coming and, filled with love and compassion ran to his son, embraced him and kissed him. God, your heavenly father, loves you that way too. He knows you have sinned greatly. He knows how rebellious you have been but He's waiting for you to come back home. He will not cast you out. He's waiting to show you love and compassion again. He is not interested in condemning you; he wants to have mercy on you.

> ***'As surely as I live, says the sovereign LORD. I take no pleasure in the death of wicked people. I only want them to turn from their wicked ways so they can live…'***
> **(Ezekiel 33:11. N.L.T)**

As we read through the rest of the prodigal son's story, we see that his father did not listen to his talk about being his servant. Instead, the best robe was placed on him; a ring was put on his fingers, and sandals on his feet. The fattened calf, which was usually reserved for very special occasions, was slaughtered and a feast to celebrate the return of the lost son began. You are valuable in the eyes of God. He does not want you to perish. He wants you back. There is no other place to be than in His loving arms. Sin will keep you from heaven; it will keep you in bondage while on earth and send you eventually to hell. But Jesus has come to set you free. If you open up your heart to Him, confess your sins and are willing to forsake them, then He will in turn save you and free you from the power of the devil.

He will give you peace and joy, the kind you have been searching for all this while. As Jesus comes into your life, He will take care of other things that trouble you. Jesus loves you. Will you accept His love?

If you will, simply confess your sins to God right now. Ask Him to forgive you and help you live a new life. Ask Jesus Christ to come into your life and help you live a godly life. Repent of, and forsake your sins. Next thing is that you continue in the study of God's word (the Bible) and fellowship with a group of Christians that will make you grow spiritually.

I CAN'T DO IT

I can't do it, I can't do it.
That has been my creed in years gone by
Each time I was on the verge of defeat
I always backed-out without a try.

But, my friend, I later learnt
That I can do anything no matter how great
Provided that on doing it, I was bent.
For life is not hinged on fate but faith.

I'll let you in on this.
It'll launch you forth if you practice it
Never ever say, 'I can't do this'
For when you do, you'll have already missed it.

'I can't' means 'I admit defeat.'
Even though the race is yet to begin.
But you probably could have achieved the feat
If you had purposed to win.

Dare to explore your abilities
You'll be amazed at what you can do
For your challenges are like keys
That open doors of promotion for you.

#KEY 5

QUIT SAYING: 'WHAT IF IT DOESN'T WORK?' IT'S BETTER TO SAY: 'WHAT IF IT WORKS?'

WHAT IF...?

It is very easy to doubt or see loopholes in any venture. Have you noticed we have more critics than achievers? There are much more pessimists than optimists. To be candid, we all have questions and doubts. But what we do with doubt is what determines our destination in life. Take advantage of doubt. Let it push you to depend on God all the more. That way, you'll overcome it. Some questions that may crop up in your mind are most likely:

- What if I fail?
- What if no one supports me?
- What if they say no?
- What if there's no money?

WHAT IF I FAIL?

You may be scared that the venture may fail; that the vision will not scale through opposition. But may I ask who gave you the vision? Remember you must first check things with God before embarking on any venture. If God is in support, then don't worry because you *cannot* fail. You may go through storms but you *will not* fail. Read Psalm 46 and be assured that God is ever with you.

And if you fail…? Then start again. Every man falls but only the great get back up. So if you fail, please know that it is not your destination. Start again and you will succeed.

WHAT IF NO ONE SUPPORTS ME?

God has always been in the business of raising people to support visions He has placed in the hearts of men. It is not your problem to know how you will be supported just pray and trust God. Do your part and let Him do His. He will not fail you. He will raise supporters. Just ask for help. Make your vision clear and unambiguous (Heb. 2:12, Isaiah 46:11, Isaiah 60).

WHAT IF THEY SAY NO?

What if I don't get the job? What if my request is refused? What if the lady turns down my proposal? What if I lose the battle? What if, what if, what if… There is really nothing worse than No. if anyone ever says 'No' to you, take courage and press on. I heard a message some time back in which the speaker said that in the midst of several Nos lies a Yes. And that single yes could turn one's life around for good. So don't be downcast because of the No. even if you lose a battle, you can still win the war.

WHAT IF THERE'S NO MONEY

God said in Psalm 50:10-12 that everything in the world belongs to Him. Psalm 24:1 tells us that the earth, its people, the things in it all belong to God. Isn't He your father? His name is Jehovah Jireh—God, the provider. Now read Matthew 7:9-11 with me:

> *'You parents—if your children ask for a loaf of bread,*
> *do you give them a stone instead? Or if they ask for fish,*
> *do you give them a snake? Of course not! If you sinful*

parents know how to give good gifts to your children, how much more will your heavenly Father give good gifts to those who ask Him.'

(N.L.T)

God will provide. Don't be afraid, just get on with the work He's committed into your hand and trust Him. Once I embarked on a project and I didn't have the money to see it through to completion. But God raised people. A woman came to where I was staying but didn't meet me. By the time I returned about 10pm, I met her waiting in the car outside. She had had a tiring day, but she still came. She even had to get someone to drive her to my place, as she was too tired to drive. When we met, she told me she had dropped some money for me with the people I was staying with. That was a big encouragement to me. I really needed money to do God's work and God had raised someone to give me some of that money. At the end of the day, other people gave money and the work was done. God raises people to support His work. God will send you help.

'May He (God) send you help from His sanctuary and strengthen you from Jerusalem.'

(Ps 20: 2 N.L.T)

Throw away the 'what ifs'. God will see you through. Next time anyone asks you: 'What if you fail?' You ask them, 'what if I succeed?' don't be deterred by the possibility of failure; be spurred-on by the greater possibility of success.

SAVING THE BEST FOR TOMORROW.

He was saving his best for tomorrow
So he didn't do his best today.
He thought to himself:
'I could always do a casual job
Today and put in my last ounce of
Strength tomorrow.'
So he kept at his work
Doing the job of an average man
All because he was saving his best for tomorrow.

But tomorrow for him never came
Because he died today.
And he died a mediocrity
The world never got to know of
His best
Because he didn't do it today.
He was saving it for tomorrow
So he died unsung, unmourned, unmissed
Because nobody knew him; nobody knows mediocrities
They only know the best.

Are you saving your best for tomorrow
And not doing your best today?
Learn to give your best today
Or else you never will.
For when tomorrow comes, there'll be another tomorrow.
For which you'll want to save your best again.
And this could go on for a whole lifetime.

Worse, tomorrow for you may never come
If you die today
Then the world will never get to know of your best
Because you didn't do it today.
You were saving it for tomorrow.
Do not die unsung, unmourned,
Unmissed and unknown.
Nobody knows the best of tomorrow,
They only know the best of today.

#KEY 6

DON'T PUT OFF UNTIL TOMORROW WHAT YOU CAN DO TODAY.

TOMORROW

'I'll do it right away.' 'I'll do it today.' These are the words typical of achievers. The words of one hungry for greatness. A lot of us are prone to saying: 'I'll do it tomorrow.' It is so convenient, so relieving. But it is detrimental to our quest for greatness. Great men act now! However, many still put off doing a lot of things till tomorrow.

- *We have not touched lives because we're waiting to do it tomorrow.*
- *We have not done that job. We are waiting for tomorrow*
- *We haven't made that visit. We are waiting for tomorrow.*
- *We have not developed our talent. We are waiting for tomorrow.*

Tomorrow never dies is the title of a movie. But as a statement, it is undeniably true. How? When tomorrow comes, there'll be another tomorrow after it. And if you and I keep up with our 'tomorrow creed', we'll never get the job done. Tomorrow never dies! Step out now! Starting a thing is half of the job done. Change your 'tomorrow song' to a 'today rhyme'. That is one hallmark of the great.

Whatever you don't do today piles up to await you tomorrow. Simple issues not resolved today become the complex matters of tomorrow. Why postpone untill tomorrow what you can do today? Procrastination is a killer of destiny. I imagine that as a result of yesterday's neglect (then, yesterday was still today) our today (which was tomorrow at that time) is now supersaturated with a legion of unresolved issues, most of which we don't even know how to start dealing with. But we can start with one, just one.

- If you have ten calls to make and you're feeling overwhelmed, start with just one. You'll feel better
- If you have ten people to visit and you feel so unfulfilled, visit one, then another. You're halfway through.
- If you have a book to read that has been so difficult for you. Start with one chapter. Beginning is half done.

The journey of a million miles begins with a step. If at the end of the day, you clear some of your backlog, you'd have moved forward appreciably. And that's how great people got where they are now. They acted one step at a time.

I believe you've learnt something. Now you're ready to go; eager to launch out, motivated to succeed. You must never forget, however, that success does not come overnight. It comes by applying principles, step by step. And as you apply them, Always remember this: *Don't put off until tomorrow what you can do today.* That, my dear friend is one of the greatest secrets of success. And it is essential wisdom, to unlock your door of greatness.

www.ingramcontent.com/pod-product-compliance
Lightning Source LLC
Chambersburg PA
CBHW051413250726
48655CB00003B/1025